THE PRINCE OF COLORED PREACHERS: CHARLES ALBERT TINDLEY

D1547637

By

E. T. TINDLEY

First Fruits Press
Wilmore, Kentucky
c2016

The Prince of Colored Preachers By E. T. Tindley

First Fruits Press, ©2016

Previously published by Shultz Printing Company, ©1942.

ISBN: 9781621714927 (print) 9781621714965 (digital) 9781621714972 (kindle)

Digital version at http://place.asburyseminary.edu/firstfruitsbooks/10/

For all other uses, contact:

First Fruits Press
B.L. Fisher Library
Asbury Theological Seminary
204 N. Lexington Ave.
Wilmore, KY 40390
http://place.asburyseminary.edu/firstfruits

Tindley, E. T.

    The prince of colored preachers: Charles Albert Tindley / by E. T. Tindley -- Wilmore, Kentucky : First Fruits Press, © 2016.

      xvi, 36 pages; 21 cm.
    Reprint. Previously published: Flint, Michigan: Shultz Printing Company, ©1942.
    ISBN: 9781621714927 (paperback)

    1. Tindley, Charles Albert. 2. Methodist Church--Clergy--Biography.
    3. Clergy--Pennsylvania--Biography. I. Title.

BX8473. T54 T55 2016   287/.632/0924

Cover design by Jonathan Ramsay

asburyseminary.edu
800.2ASBURY
204 North Lexington Avenue
Wilmore, Kentucky 40390

First Fruits Press
The Academic Open Press of Asbury Theological Seminary
204 N. Lexington Ave., Wilmore, KY 40390
859-858-2236
first.fruits@asburyseminary.edu
asbury.to/firstfruits

CHARLES ALBERT TINDLEY, D.D.

Dedicated to

*The many friends
Doctor Tindley made
during his lifetime
and to all who will
take Christ as their
Saviour and Guide.*

by

The Authors

PROF. AND MRS. E. T. TINDLEY

Printed in U. S. A.

by the

SCHULTZ PRINTING COMPANY
Flint, Michigan

THE PRINCE OF
COLORED PREACHERS

The Remarkable Story of
CHARLES ALBERT TINDLEY
Of Philadelphia, Pennsylvania

Copyright 1942
by
PROF. E. T. TINDLEY

PRICE TWENTY-FIVE CENTS

Introduction
by
FRANK S. HEMINGWAY
Mgr. of Radio Station
WMPC
Lapeer, Michigan

For additional copies of this book
write

W. E. COLE
Distributor of Christian Literature
Bentley Street   Lapeer, Michigan

INTRODUCTION

The colored folks have given the world many illustrious names such as, Booker T. Washington, Paul Lawrence Dunbar, Amanda Smith, George Washington Carver and not least among these is the name of Charles Albert Tindley D.D. lovingly called "The Prince of Colored Preachers."

One of his friends paid tribute to him in the following words: "Dr. Tindley is one of the most loved men of his race. He is a veritable giant, six feet two, weighing two hundred thirty pounds, rugged, honest, humble, compassionate. There is about him a simplicity and dignity of soul that suggests the thought of 'A Lincoln in ebony', as the white friends of Tindley have designated him. When Bennett college gave him the degree of Doctor of Divinity, he said, 'I am still a humble student endeavoring to improve myself every day.'

"He is full of quaint wisdom. When he took his examination for the ministry he was sexton of the church that he afterwards returned to serve as pastor for more than thirty years and to build into the great Tindley Temple. At the time of the examination a bumptious colored man, a college graduate who was also to take the examination contemptuously inquired of Tindley, 'How do you expect to pass this examination? I and the other candidates hold diplomas in our hands. What do you hold?' 'Nothing but a broom', replied Tindley who had just left sweeping. Tindley passed second among a large class of candidates all of whom were school men.

"A prominent white Philadelphian said of him, 'The man is an inspiration; his very soul sings.' Out of this life of pathos and sunshine, of struggle and achievement have come such cheering and comforting songs as: 'I'll Overcome Some Day,' 'We'll Understand It Better By and By,' 'Go Wash in That Beautiful Stream,' and ' What Are They Doing in Heaven Today?'

The record of his life is an inspiration to all classes of people. The courage and determination with which he faced the trials and difficulties of early life will help all who have to travel the way of adversity. The modest unassuming spirit with which he met world-wide fame as an outstanding preacher, lecturer, leader, and song writer is a lesson in humility for every Christian. At a time when his Sunday School was the largest in Methodism, his church membership one of the largest in the world, and he was preaching regularly to "standing room only" congregations three times each Sunday, in answer to a questionnaire he ascribed his success not to natural attributes but to A GREAT ENDUEMENT OF THE HOLY SPIRIT.

Another deeply inspiring phase of his life is the example of child-like faith with which he carried his many heavy burdens to the Lord, prayed through seemingly insurmountable difficulties, and obtained practical wisdom to build and lead a church having at the time of his death TWELVE THOUSAND FIVE HUNDRED members, an assistant pastor and forty-nine local preachers.

The poems at the close of each of the chapters of this book have been taken from a collection of his writings entitled NEW SONGS OF PARADISE which have been a great blessing and help to many people. One of the most precious paragraphs to be included in this chapter of introduction is, that now, a decade after his homegoing, all six of Dr. Tindley's surviving children are Christians and still associated in Christian work. The youngest son, Prof. Elbert T. Tindley, upon whom his father prayed his mantle might fall is carrying on, in an evangelistic ministry singing his father's heartfelt songs of the Gospel to many congregations throughout the land.

Dr. Tindley's remarkable ministry is a modern miracle of the grace of God. It began in the experience described in one of his own favorite songs,

I HAVE FOUND AT LAST, A SAVIOUR

> *I have found at last the Saviour,*
> *Of whom I've often heard,*
> *And I have the precious favor,*
> *He has promised in His word:*
> *Oh the joy that comes to me,*
> *And the pow'r makes me free,*
> *My soul is filled with praises,*
> *'Tis the year of jubilee.*
> *I have promised I would follow,*
> *However rough the way,*
> *Leaving all things of tomorrow,*
> *I will trust Him just today:*
> *For the morning doth appear,*
> *Which will banish ev'ry fear,*
> *I shall see the land of Beulah,*
> *With my eyes undimmed by tears.*

THE BOY WITH THE BARE FEET

Charles Albert Tindley was born on the eastern shore of Maryland, in the small town of Berlin, Worcester County, July 7, 1851. He was born in slavery and when about the age of five years, soon after his mother's death, was separated from his father, taken to the little town of Genesa, Maryland, where he was held in slavery. There in an old-fashioned brick house which faced the Chesapeake Bay, this young Negro boy grew up among strangers, and as it must have appeared to him, in a new and strange world. The people who then owned him proved to be very cruel, and would not permit him to have a book nor to go to church.

When he would find bits of old newspapers while walking along the roadside, he would pick them up and put them in his bosom as he had no pockets, in order to study each letter after everyone had retired. At times during the day he would gather pine knots, and when the people were asleep, would light these pine knots. Then with the poor light these burning knots would afford him he would use fire coals as pencils and would mark all the words he could make out on the bits of newspapers he had collected, lying flat on his stomach to prevent being seen by any one who might still be about. A young white lad about the same age as Tindley, became very chummy with him, and was his only teacher in his struggle for an education. This white boy was Calvin B. Taylor who later became Berlin, Maryland's leading banker. This method of procuring an education was so crude that Tindley was seventeen years of age before he could spell out the word "cat." He continued in this way, however, until he could read the Bible almost without stopping to spell the words.

There was a growing desire within the breast of Charles A. Tindley to go to church. On Saturday morning he would go down to the Chesapeake Bay, and with ashes he would wash his only shirt in the Bay, hang it on the limb of a tree, and then would stand in the shade of the trees to keep the hot sun from his bare back until his shirt was dry enough to put on. This Saturday wash took place with the hope that on Sunday he could go to church. One Sunday, after he had driven the cattle to pasture, an uncontrollable impulse came urging him to go to church. He had no shoes nor coat to wear; his pants, if such as he had on could be described as that, were or had been tow linen. He had patched them as best he could. With this outfit including the shirt he had washed the day before, though not ironed nor very clean, he started to the church, praying all the way for the chance to slip up into the gallery without being seen, and hide behind some boxes that were stored there, and in that way could hear the sermon. When he was approaching the church he began to think of himself in the light of fitness to enter a church on Sunday. The first thing he discovered to be out of order for the Lord's House, was his bare feet. They seemed larger than ever and were not clean. He proceeded to wash them in a ditch that contained a little water, then dried them with a handful of leaves and continued to church. He remained contented behind the boxes until the speaker, who was a Missionary, called for all the boys and girls who could read the Bible to come to the front. One big lump after another arose in his throat as he thought of what he should do. Wasn't he one who could read the Bible? No one in the Church knew that but himself, so he rolled up a big resolution and started down from the gallery. The church was that of a white congregation, and there is no need to say that this action came very near breaking up the morning service. The people hissed and cleared their throats and did many other things to get his attention, but with eyes on the speaker he made right for the front, and the Missionary, a true ambassador of the Lord, permitted him to come on and wait his turn to read the lesson. When the lesson was read he returned to his place in the gallery, but not to hide, for all the people were watching and whispering about the "boy with the bare feet."

IT MAY BE THE BEST FOR ME

I often wonder why it is,
   While some are happy and free,
That I am tired and sore oppressed,
   But it may be the best for me.

Some walk in paths with flowers strewn
   No burdens, no misery,
While I must bear my cross alone,
   But it may be the best for me.

GOD WILL PROVIDE

From that first experience in church, his ambition to be educated knew no bounds. He would plow all day in the field and in the evening would walk and run fourteen miles going and coming, to get to the school teacher who was kind enough to give him lessons. Through such methods and means he obtained information until he was able to leave Maryland to go to Philadelphia.

After his arrival in Philadelphia, he became employed by a building contractor as a hod carrier and for slightly over three years he worked at that job during the day and studied as much as he could at night. During this same time he was sexton of the old Bainbridge M. E. store front Mission on Bainbridge Street below Twelfth Street in Philadelphia. He had made up his mind to learn at least one new thing—a thing he did not know the day before—each day. He kept that rule until his death. In 1880 he was married to Anna Daisy Henry, and to this union there were born twelve children, six boys and six girls. With every dollar he could spare he would buy a book that would help fit him to pass the examination for the ministry, of which he was successful in 1885, and was admitted on trial in the Delaware Conference, of the Methodist Episcopal Church. By correspondence, he entered all the schools which his limited means would afford, and sought to keep up the studies with any pupil who studied in the school room. He was able to attend the Brandywine Institute and to finish its Theological course. By correspondence he took the Greek course through the Boston Theological School and the Hebrew under Professor Speaker through the Hebrew Synagogue on North Broad Street in Philadelphia, Pa. He took studies in Science and Literature as a private student because he was unable to attend the Universities where these subjects were taught. Thus while he was unable to go through the schools, he was able to let the school go through him.

He was sent to Cape May, New Jersey, to take over his first appointment and it was here that one of the greatest experiences of his life took place. Cape May was experiencing a heavy snow storm and in a humble cottage around the dining room table were a mother and father and in two high chairs were a small girl and boy, waiting to be given their morning food. It was the home of the new preacher, Charles A. Tindley and his family. They had no food except a stale piece of bread, and had decided to dip that in some water, for they had no milk, soften it up a bit, then break it into pieces to give to Mary and Fredrick. As for themselves, they were not going to eat anything. In the front room was another baby daughter who had passed away the night before. Her name was Elanora, and having no funds with which to bury her, they were faced with a problem.

Charles Tindley asked his wife to set the table as though she had the food to put in the dishes. She was reluctant to do so at first but finally she agreed. After the table had been set, he said, "Now let us get on our knees and have our morning prayer." He thanked God for being alive, for their health and strength, for the sunshine and the snow storm that was raging outside. Not once did he complain about the shortage of provisions, but thanked God for what they had. Then getting up from their knees and seating themselves at the table, and while in the attitude of saying grace over the food that was not there, surely that was faith, for in Hebrews 11:1 we read: "Faith is the substance of things hoped for, the evidence of things not seen", they heard a man commanding his team of horses, "Whoa! Whoa!" Then getting out and coming up to the house, kicking his boots against the sill of the door to get the snow off, he hollered, "Hey! is anybody alive here?" Getting up from the table and going to the door to answer the call, Charles Tindley beheld a white gentleman with a large sack of provisions on his shoulder. Slinging it down to the floor he said: "Knowing you were the new parson here, and not knowing how you were making out in this storm, my wife and I thought you might need some food. I've a cartload of wood out here, too. I'll dump it and be on my way."

Tindley with tears streaming down his face, thanked the man and said to him, "You are an answer to prayer, for we didn't have anything to eat except a stale crust of bread, and had decided to dip that in water to soften it up and give to the children. Our daughter, Elanora, is in the front room dead, and we haven't the means to bury her. We are not going to worry though, for we know God will provide a way."

The man was surprised and shocked to learn that there was a girl dead and he said, "Don't worry. I'll have to go now, but I'll be back and see to it that your child has a decent burial."

It was during the night of that same day after everyone had gone to bed, seated in a rocker thinking over the blessings of the day, he was inspired to write the song: "God Will Provide For Me."

GOD WILL PROVIDE FOR ME

Here I may be weak and poor,
With afflictions to endure;
All about me not a ray of light to see,
Just as He has often done,
For His helpless trusting ones,
God has promised to provide for me.

All my raiment and my food,
And my health and all that's good;
Are within His own written guarantee,
God is caring for the poor,
Just as He has done before,
He has promised to provide for me.

God has promised to provide for me;
God has promised to provide for me;
All creation is His own,
All my needs to Him are known.
He has promised to provide for me.

THE LORD WILL MAKE THE WAY

After serving Cape May, New Jersey, for two years, his next appointment to a church was in Odessa, Delaware. Because God had so miraculously blessed his ministry on his first charge, he went forth to fill his second with a stronger determination not knowing he was to again encounter another great experience. Charles Tindley, six feet two inches tall and very slender, had been suffering with a lung condition that caused him to have hemorrhages after each sermon. He tried to conceal this from his family as much as possible, stating each time it occurred that it was simply a case of overtaxation on his throat, and wasn't anything to worry over. Secretly it did worry him for he realized that each time he suffered from a hemorrhage, it left him weaker than before, and if this continued, he'd soon collapse. One Monday morning, after a restless night and feeling discouraged over his condition, he decided to end it all in preference of becoming a burden to his family. Kissing them all goodbye as was his custom when he left the house to take care of his pastorial duties, he went out into the woods, and seating himself beneath a tree began sharpening his pocket-knife. His attention was attracted by a bird singing up in the same tree under which he was seated. Forgetting his troubles for the moment, he began talking to the bird. Suddenly he realized that the bird had not a soul like himself, nor a heaven to go to when death came, yet could be so happy and sing so beautifully, that he became ashamed of himself for being a coward and not having enough faith in his heavenly Father whenever trials came upon him. Putting away his knife, he began to pray for forgiveness and if he had been called to preach the Gospel, to heal him of this illness.

Getting to his feet he walked slowly out of the woods, wondering how close he had come to committing an unpardonable sin if it had not been for the singing of that bird. He was not aware of the direction in which he was going until he discovered he was near the home of a Homeopathic Doctor and was impressed to go in. He asked the doctor to fill a prescription. Then proceeded to advise him what to mix. The doctor looked at him very strangely and asked who gave him such a prescription and refused to fill it unless he signed his name and address, releasing him from all blame if anything should happen. He signed the release, the prescription was filled and the medicine healed him completely. He tried many times to remember the prescription he had asked for that day, but could not. Without doubt it was given to him for that particular time ONLY. Out of this experience was born the song: "The Lord Will Make The Way."

The hills of life which you must climb,
Each moment, day by day,
Are rough; the path is hard to find,
But God will make the way.

And when the dreary road you tread,
Which leads to endless day,
O praise the Lord, there'll be no dread,
For Christ will be the way.

HE'LL TAKE YOU THROUGH

After serving Odessa, Delaware for two years, he was sent to what was then a two-point circuit called, Pocomoke Circuit, Maryland. For three years he remained on this charge, working zealously night and day to bring the charge up to where it should be. He was able to demolish the old church building in Unionville, and erect in its place a new structure. Twenty miles away in a little village that had somehow forgotten to be named was located his other charge. Because they hadn't a church building, arrangements were made for them to hold their services in the school house on Sundays. However, this did not suit their pastor, and it wasn't long before plans were on the way for a church building. After the church was completed, it was unanimously voted to name it "Tindley Chapel." Strange to say, a few years later the village was given the same name, and to this day is known as Tindley Chapel.

From 1892 to 1895, he was stationed at Fairmount, Maryland. By this time most of the people on the eastern shore of Maryland had sometime or other heard of or attended his services. To many he had become known as "The tall, lanky, silver-tongued pulpit orator."

In 1896 he was appointed Presiding Elder (now known as District Superintendent), but after one year, prefering the pastorate instead, was sent to Exion M. E. Church, Wilmington, Delaware. After serving these people for five years, in the spring of 1902, when the Delaware Annual Conference convened at Janes Street

M. E. Church, Germantown, Pennsylvania, he was appointed to what was then known as Old Bainbridge Street M. E. Church, in Philadelphia, Pennsylvania.

This church was located on Bainbridge Street below Twelfth, and was only a store-front building with a congregation numbering between thirty-five and forty. The pastors who had served there up to this time of Tindley's appointment, had been men with University Degrees, but somehow they had not succeeded. Many remembering him from the time he was admitted to the Conference, wondered if he wasn't making a big mistake, for if men of Letters failed before him—surely he hadn't a chance. Charles Tindley did not allow these things to upset him, but entered his new task with unfailing faith in God, believing all things were possible with those who put their trust in HIM.

The congregation began to grow steadily, until the old store-front building was replaced by a brownstone-front church with a seating capacity of six hundred. It was later remodeled, and a horse-shoe gallery added two hundred more seats, bringing the seating capacity total to eight hundred. Every Sunday morning people would come early in order to get a seat to hear this tall, humble man of God preach, until the church was crowded to the doors, and many, failing to even find standing space were turned away. The membership continued to increase with such rapidity that it became a problem to the pastor and officials as to what to do. Tindley, realizing the answer must come from God, went to his knees in prayer.

HE'LL TAKE YOU THROUGH

Lifetime is like a single day,
　Through which we mortals make our way.
We move from morning's youth to noon,
　And then to ev'ning all so soon.

Before your life is well begun,
　The earthly task is almost done;
Your space below—so short, so brief,
　Leaves not much time for joy or grief.

On swiftly speeds this nature-train,
　Through tunnels dark, o'er desert plain,
Where trestles span the deep ravine;
　Where tow'ring mountain peaks are seen.

When light'nings flash across your track,
　And nature tried to keep you back,
Within His care you are secure,
　Your guide has been this way before.

No accident has been His fate,
　His train has never came in late,
All signals show the track is clear,
　The passengers have naught to fear.

A few more stations, and we'll be,
　From toil and care and danger free.
O could we render praises due,
　To Christ, the one who takes us through.

If you take Jesus for your guide,
　You'll find HIM more than all beside,
Just do the things HE bids you do,
　He'll take you through, He'll take you through.

WE'LL UNDERSTAND IT BETTER
BY AND BY

It was not until the year of 1907 that he, being led by the Holy spirit, crossed over on Broad and Fitzwater Streets to procure the old Westminister Presbyterian Church, a property that cost $69,000. The members of the board of Trustees were not in harmony with this move, knowing that Broad Street was one of the main streets in Philadelphia and that heretofore, no other Colored church had ever been on that street. Some thought it was a foolish move their pastor had made, thus causing the Board of Trustees to split and sending their pastor to the Douglas Hospital suffering with a bleeding heart. When he was able to resume his duties at the church, he discovered a rival faction headed by the president of the Trustee Board had been organized to hinder any plans he might suggest for the advancement of the church. He had to be very careful how he handled such a grave situation realizing if he lost his self-control and fought back, it would be to their satisfaction, for not only his character would be ruined but he would lose ground and the sight of his goal. So he decided not to say a word but to continually pray that God would take hold of the situation, and if he had been· obedient to His plans then clear away all the stumps that might be found in his path, and let the faithful few go through to victory. Not only did he pray this prayer secretly in his home but whenever the clouds seemed dense and the load heavy, he would suddenly fall to his knees behind the sacred desk, to the amazement of the congregation, and again implore God to clear the way.

Not long afterwards, death rode through that church with lightning speed, and the first whose cup of iniquity had been filled and time called, was none other than the president of the Trustee Board. This created a great commotion not only in that particular church, but throughout the city, for he was widely known among the fraternal organizations. However, this was only the beginning, for in a few days others followed in succession until the remaining members of that faction became alarmed the moment their pastor began to pray. Some one later on suggested a dinner be given in honor of the pastor and his wife and in this way enable them to get rid of him. In due time the invitation was received. Somehow he realized what was in their minds, but did not mention it to his wife until the day of the occasion, when he suggested that she remain at home and he would make a proper excuse for her, because he was afraid of what might happen.

When he arrived at the home where the dinner was to be served, he discovered they had two chairs beautifully decorated for himself and his wife and that each one had their respective plates served but himself. After he had blessed the table a woman brought in his plate nicely fixed on a tray and set it before him. Not wanting to arouse their suspicion, he made pretense of eating around the edge of his plate, then suddenly looking at his watch; asked to be excused for an engagement he had to attend. In the first drug store he came to, he purchased something to counteract any poison that might have gotten into his system.

We are tossed and driven on the restless sea of time.
Sombre skies and howling tempest oft' succeeds a
*   bright sunshine,*
In that land of perfect day, when the mist have
*   roll'd away,*
We will understand it better by and by.

We are often destitute of the things that life demands,
Want of shelter and of food-thirsty hills and barren
*   lands,*
We are trusting in the Lord, and according to His
*   word,*
We will understand it better by and by.

Trials dark on ev'ry hand, and we cannot understand,
All the ways that God would lead us to the Blessed
*   Promis'd Land,*
But He guides us with His eye, and we'll follow 'til
*   we die,*
For we'll understand it better by and by.

Temptations, hidden snares, often take us unawares,
And our hearts are made to bleed for a thoughtless
*   Word or deed,*
And we wonder why the test, when we try to do our
*   best;*
But we'll understand it better by and by.

By and by, when the morning comes,
All the saints of God are gathered home,
We'll tell the story how we've overcome,
For we'll understand it better by and by.

LET JESUS FIX IT FOR YOU

The name of the church was changed from Bainbridge Street M. E., to Calvary M. E., but because it was discovered that another Calvary M. E. Church was located in West Philadelphia, they decided to name it East Calvary M. E. Church. The membership increased as the years went by, until at ten o'clock each Sunday morning, the main auditorium would be crowded and the lower auditorium was opened to take care of the overflow. The pastor preached upstairs, and his assistant downstairs. Many times students from the different schools of religion in and about Philadelphia would attend the services and take notes.

The Watch Meeting services were always the beginning of their winter revivals which aften ran into the month of February resulting in hundreds being saved. Noticing during the cold winter months men and women without the proper clothing and food, some even without shelter, Tindley's heart would go out to them, and remembering the hardships he had experienced in his earlier life, he wanted to extend a helping hand to all who came that way, regardless of their race, color or creed. What a picture that must have made to the pedestrians on Broad Street: a long line of humanity waiting to be clothed and fed. This work was carried on year after year without any expense to the church, but from his own personal funds. One night during the protracted meetings and after a large group of unfortunates had been cared for through the day, the pastor having finished his message, extended the invitation to accept Christ, which resulted in a large number responding. Among the number was a young white man in his early twenties, and the pastor came to him and asked him his name and how he felt about his soul. After he had answered, the pastor asked him where he was from as his name was familiar. He said he was from Maryland. Then the pastor asked him what part of Maryland? The answer was, "Eastern Shore." Charles Tindley told him he was from the Eastern Shore also, and wanted to know what part he was from. The answer was, "Genesa." Pastor Tindley then asked him to face the audience and said, "Friends, you are now looking in the face of the grand-son of the man who was my owner in slavery." Then he quoted: "God moves in a mysterious way, His wonders to perform. He plants His footsteps in the sea and rides upon the storm." The audience took up this hymn with a hum. When they had finished, Tindley assured the young man he was among friends and need not be uneasy.

Because of his long stay and continued success as pastor of the Philadelphia church, some of the brethren of the conference became envious and began to question his ability to handle such a large church, knowing he did not have a college education. It wasn't long before these rumors reached him. One day he asked his wife to pack a few things as he had a short trip to make. He went to Bennet College located in Greensboro, North Carolina, and asked the President if arrangements could be made to give him the course in

Theology as soon as possible. It usually takes four years to complete this course, but after two days Charles Tindley was able to leave the college with his diploma as a testimony of his efficiency.

If your life in days gone by,
Has not been good and true,
In your own way no longer try,
But let Him fix it for you.

Perhaps your temper is to blame,
For many wrongs you do,
Take it to God in Jesus' name,
And He will fix it for you.

If in your home the trouble is
The course you should pursue,
To talk with God, your hand in His,
And He will fix it for you.

And if some sin your soul hath bound
With cords you can't undo,
At Jesus' feet go lay it down,
And He will fix it for you.

Maybe to you the world is dark,
And comforts far and few,
Let Jesus own and rule your heart,
And He wll fix it for you.

Let Jesus fix it for you,
He knows just what to do;
Whenever you pray, let Him have His way,
And He will fix it for you.

TAKE YOUR BURDEN TO THE LORD

Charles A. Tindley was busily engaged in his study one morning, when he was told that a man wished to see him. After the man had been admitted, he was asked to state his mission. He told of his heavy burdens which were becoming more than he could bear thus seeking his council and advice. Pastor Tindley having many times been confronted with this same situation, advised him, "Go home and secure a large sack, then get all of your troubles together and name each one as you drop them in, to be sure that none is forgotten. Get it up on your shoulder and go upstairs away from everyone. When this is done, sling that burden down at the feet of Jesus, and leave it there. As you go about your daily work, thank Him for answering your prayer, and before you realize it—your prayer will be answered." After the man had left, Charles Tindley composed the song entitled: "Take Your Burden to the Lord and Leave It There."

The church was never closed. During the day people would often stop on their way for rest and prayer. The congregation grew until the church became too small. Prayer meetings were held on each Tuesday night and were attended by 800 to 1600 persons. They were REAL prayer meetings. The kind that are now out of date, but NO CHURCH CAN BE ANY GREATER THAN IT'S PRAYER MEETING.

It was not long before pastor Tindley got the vision of a new and larger church to take care of his members. Knowing that some time ago the present church had been paid for, and this new project could be accomplished without hurting anyone financially. Five buildings next to the church were bought and soon demolished. A few months later, the new building was finished and paid for through the tithes of the members. No suppers, no bazaars, no auctions or rummage sales, no block parties or church carnivals, no ticket selling no pinning on of the donkey's tail. Just simple tithing paid for that structure that cost $350,000. The four manuel organ at a cost of $40,000 was also paid for.

The men were placing the chairs and furniture about, getting ready for the great opening the next day which was Sunday, December 7, 1924. Pastor Charles Tindley, together with his wife, went over to the church to watch and admire every nook and corner of the church, which was to them the greatest achievement for the advancement of the Gospel of Jesus Christ in their ministry. Smilingly she turned to her husband and said, "Well, at last it is finished and I'm so happy." On returning home, she prepared the meal for the next day, for she wanted to spend the entire day at the church. She was well and hearty until five minutes after twelve o'clock midnight when she took sick with acute indigestion. She passed on within thirty minutes. After faithfully standing by her husband for forty-five years, she slipped quietly away.

The seating capacity of the new church is 3,200 and at the time of its completion, the membership numbered a little more than 10,000.

Many times on Sunday mornings, two services were held. The first at ten o'clock and the other at eleven. Often request was made that the congregation would not return for the evening service, so as to allow those who could not get in at the morning service, a chance to attend. The old church was now used entirely for rescue work.

If the world from you with-hold of its silver and its gold,

And you have to get along with meagre fare,

Just remember, in His word, how He feeds the little bird,

Take your burden to the Lord and leave it there.

If your body suffers pain, and your health you can't regain,

And your soul is almost sinking in despair,

Jesus knows the pain you feel, He can save and He can heal,

Take your burden to the Lord and leave it there.

When your enemies assail, and your heart begins to fail,

Don't forget that God in heaven answers pray'r

He will make a way for you and will lead you safely through,

Take your burden to the Lord and leave it there.

When your youthful days are gone, and old age is stealing on,

And your body bends beneath the weight of care,

He will never leave you then, He'll go with you to the end,

Take your burden to the Lord and leave it there.

NOTHING BETWEEN

Charles Tindley never took a vacation from his work and unless he was out of the city, could be always found at the church. Even on Saturday nights he taught all who would come, one hour Bible lessons. This was known as the Saturday Night Bible Class. During the summer months, after he had finished his preaching services on Sunday night, he would go down on his farm in Colman, Maryland, to spend the week in retreat and meditation, in preparation for his sermon of the next Sunday. While working on his sermon on July 2, 1933, he felt the strength going slowly from his body. He realized what was taking place so he called to his wife Jennie (for he had married again in 1927), and asked her to get his clothes together and inform Buster, the boy who drove the car, to get it in shape because he was going home. She was not alarmed, for she thought he had a business engagement in Philadelphia. However, when they had arrived in Philadelphia, he asked to be taken to the Douglas hospital instead of the parsonage On entering the hospital he met the head physician, Dr. McDougall, and said, "Dr. McDougall, I want the same room I had in 1907 when I was suffering with a bleeding heart." At first the Doctor thought he was jesting, but Tindley, holding up his hand said, "I am not fooling, I'm serious. This is just as good a place to go to heaven from as any place I know." After seeing his wife and Buster with the bags on the elevator, he decided to walk up the three flights of stairs. When he had arrived in his room, undressed himself, and laid down on the bed, he instructed his wife to get in touch with his six children (three boys and three girls), and not to bring him any mail pertaining to the church, for his work there had been finished.

He had a week to talk to his children, taking them by turn beginning with the oldest. It was the day before his death that his youngest child was admitted. Waiting until the rest had left, he turned over on his side and said, "Son, take a seat by the window, I want to talk to you. Will you believe your old dad when he tells you as he lays on this cot, that there is NOTHING BETWEEN MY SOUL AND MY SAVIOR? NOT A STAIN OR SIN ANYWHERE AROUND ME, NOT A STAIN OF SIN INSIDE OF ME?" Then looking out of the window where his son was seated, and pointing with his index finger, continued, "I can see my mansion now, it is as large as the state of Pennsylvania." The deeds of each day are as material being sent up to God to be placed on our mansion. Great was the mansion that Dr. Tindley saw for himself. What is the size of YOUR mansion?

He said other things to his youngest son that are sacred and will never be known to mortals, and admonished him to stick close to the church of God and to keep the name Tindley unspotted and high in the religious world. Then with tears streaming down his cheeks and those of his son, they solemnly sealed their pledge with a hand clasp, as he lifted his face heavenward and prayed God would keep his son in the center of His will.

Thus he threw the mantle of his ministry upon the shoulders of his youngest child with faith that God could and would use him.

Nothing between my soul and the Saviour,
* Naught of this world's delusive dream,*
I have renounced all sinful pleasure,
* Jesus is mine; there's nothing between.*

Nothing between like worldly pleasure,
* Habits of life though harmless they seem,*
Must not my heart from Him ever sever,
* He is my all, there's nothing between.*

Nothing between, like pride or station,
* Self or friends shall not intervene,*
Though it may cost me much tribulation,
* I am resolved, there's nothing between.*

Nothing between, e'en many hard trials,
* Though the whole world against me convene;*
Watching with pray'r and much self denial,
* I'll triumph at last, with nothing between.*

Nothing between my soul and the Saviour,
* So that His blessed face may be seen,*
Nothing preventing the least of His favor,
* Keep the way clear! let nothing between.*

GOING UPSTAIRS

Dr. Tindley requested that there be no sadness shown at his funeral. He wanted lots of flowers of which he was a great lover. Rather than a funeral, he wanted it conducted as a farewell reception, where all of the hymns he composed would be sung, especially the one entitled "The Home Of The Soul," (he began singing it and on reaching the high note in the song, he paused and said), "When you reach this high note, if you should happen to hear a strange noise, don't become alarmed but look up, for it will be me leading the heavenly choir." He also requested that the person in charge would extend an invitation to those who would wish to dedicate themselves to Christ for "I would like to present my Savior a bouquet of human lives at my farewell reception."

The next day the hospital room was crowded with the immediate family together with doctors and nurses of the hospital staff. As Dr. Tindley was talking to them, Doctor Turner an attending physician, came into the room to inform Dr. Tindley that there was a large group from his church outside the hospital praying that God would raise him up so that he might come back and preach to them. Dr. Tindley smiled for he was very happy over the thought that the people he had ministered to so long appreciated him as much as that.

Then turning to his wife, and holding on to her hand, he said with emphasis, "Jennie, didn't I tell you when I leave here I'm going straight from here to heaven?" She tried to calm him by saying, "Yes, Charles, but you must try to be quiet." Laying there smiling at all in the room, he repeated in a stronger voice than before, "Jennie, I told you when I die I'm going straight from here to heaven." Again she begged him not to get excited. Gazing around the room at all assembled there, he smiled as if pronouncing a benediction on them, and looking up into his wife's face for the last time he said, "I told you when I die I was going straight from here (pointing with his index finger to the bed on which he was lying) to heaven and I'm going—NOW." Straightening himself out on the bed, and placing a beautiful smile on his face that never wore off, "WENT UPSTAIRS." (This was his expression as to a Christian's passing away to be with the Lord). He surely had NOTHING BETWEEN HIS SOUL AND HIS SAVIOUR.

I hear of a city, a heavenly home,
Where sorrows and dangers and strife never come,
Where the walls are of jasper, and the streets pav'd
with gold.
That city is Heaven, the home of the soul.

The saints up in Heaven, they weep not or sigh,
Or say to their loved ones the mournful goodbye,
But happy forever in the city of gold,
The city is Heaven, the home of the soul.

No sin is in Heaven, no uncleanness there,
For Satan can't enter that city so fair,
The King in His beauty the saints shall behold,
In the city of Heaven, the home of the soul.

CHRIST THE WAY

Charles Albert Tindley departed this life July 26, 1933 at the age of 82 years. His body was brought into the church Sunday night, July 30th at 6 o'clock and there remained in state until noon Monday, July 31st. A steady stream of humanity of many races and from all walks of life passed by in silent tribute for eighteen hours to show respect to this man of God.

Five thousand persons jammed Tindley Methodist Temple to witness the funeral services which began at 1:00 P.M. At the request of Bishop Richardson, Presiding Bishop of the Philadelphia area, who was on the high sea enroute to Europe, Dr. D. W. Henry, District Superintendent, was in charge of the service. As in keeping with Dr. Tindley's request, the three great choirs sang alternately the hymns he composed.

Representatives from all denominations throughout the country were in attendance, beside civil leaders from city and state. As many as time permitted of the telegrams, cables, and letters of consolences that were received were read.

Out of the esteem and respect for the long number of years that Pastor Tindley served in the city of Philadelphia the radio stations WDAS and WPEN broadcast the service in its entirety in relays which lasted five hours.

Before the close of the service Dr. Henry extended an invitation to all those who wished to present themselves to God as a living sacrifice. It was a beautiful sight to see young and old standing around Dr. Tindley's bier. Then the services were closed. On the outside of the Temple stood many thousands who were not able to get in, and as the casket was borne to the hearse some one in the crowd was heard to say: "Our friend is gone, what will we do this winter." (Dr. Tindley for years fed and clothed the unfortunate. No doubt this person had been one of those and was wondering what would become of them the following winter.) There were over 300 cars in the procession preceded by 12 cars of flowers, headed by a police escort which wended its way to the Eden Cemetery, where the body was interred in the family burial plot.

Dr. Tindley left a congregation of over 12,500 members, made up of representatives of every nationality in the world. It was through the kindness of his friend who was (at the time the new church was built in 1924), his Presiding Bishop, the late Joseph F. Berry, that the name of the church was changed to "TINDLEY TEMPLE M. E. CHURCH." He was retained as pastor in Philadelphia, Pennsylvania, for 32 years. He was Ministerial delegate to the General Conference from 1908 through 1932. More than once he was a candidate for the Bishopry, the highest office in the Methodist Episcopal Church, but always withdrew, preferring to remain a pastor.

He acquired a library of 4,000 volumes. Beside his desk stood his prayer altar and next to it was a lounge. Every morning about four o'clock he would leave his bed room, and enter his library to pray for strength, knowledge and guidance of the Holy Spirit to lead his people. After spending much time in prayer he would lie down on the lounge to rest still in the attitude of prayer. Many have asked the secret of Dr. Charles A. Tindley's success. It can only be attributed to the TIME HE SPENT ON HIS KNEES—ALONE WITH GOD, taking Christ as his way of life which he expressed so beautifully in the following hymn.

Christ the way; in exaltation:
 Though He stands on heights aflame.
Glorious in transfiguration,
 He is always meek the same.

Christ the way; in self denial;
 Fasting in the wilderness.
He endured the tempter's trial,
 Stood unmoved, the three fold test.

Christ the way; when others wrong'd Him;
 Though He had not done amiss.
Judas, with pretended virtue,
 Sold his Master for a kiss.

Christ the way; amid afflictions;
 Cursed and bruised in Pilate's hall.
False accused and contradictions,
 Lamb of God, He bore it all.

He is the way to perfect salvation,
 He is the way to mansions above,
He is the first of the new creation,
 Pattern of truth and fullness of love.

Write

W. E. COLE

Distributor of Christian Literature

Bentley Street, Lapeer, Michigan

for

following publications

"New Songs of Paradise No. 6"	*Tindley*	$ .50
"Today in Bible Prophecy"	*Buroker*	.25
"Today in Bible Prophecy No. 2"	*Buroker*	.25
"Yesterday in Bible Prophecy"	*Buroker*	.25
"Seven Pillars of Civilization"	*Buroker*	.25
"C. England of Lapeer"	*Buroker*	.25
"The Scripture Cannot Be Broken"	*Didier*	.10
"The Blood of the Lamb"	*Didier*	.10
"Search the Scriptures"	*Didier*	.10
"The Word of His Power"	*Didier*	.10
"Faith Which Worketh By Love"	*Didier*	.10
"Ye Must Be Born Again"	*Didier*	.10
"The Time Is At Hand"	*Didier*	.10
"We Shall Live Again" (Poems)	*Augsbury*	.25
"The Great Apostle"	*Cross*	.25
"101 Devotional Bible Readings"	*Dean*	.25
"Know Your Bible Radio Hour"—No. 1		.25
"Who Am I" Children's Radio Bible Hour		.25

Made in United States
North Haven, CT
19 March 2022

17302713R00026